TAKING
TESTS

THE A+ GUIDE TO

TAKING TESTS

LOUISE COLLIGAN

SCHOLASTIC BOOK SERVICES
New York Toronto London Auckland Sydney Tokyo

ISBN 0-590-32186-2

Copyright © 1982 by Louise Colligan.
All rights reserved. Published by Scholastic Book Services, a division of Scholastic Inc.

12 11 10 9 8 7 6 5 4 3 2 1   1   2 3 4 5 6 7/8

Printed in the U.S.A.   06

To my mother, Bernice Hogan

TABLE OF CONTENTS

Chapter 1

HOW TO GET TEST-WISE

The class bell has just rung. You look around the room. A lot of students look as though they forgot to go to bed last night. Two or three of them look bug-eyed and twitchy, probably from drinking too much coffee during the night. You hear a lot of nervous paper-shuffling. A couple of students are trying to decipher the scrawl on small, wrinkled scraps of paper. A few others are flipping frantically through their notebooks and textbooks, which have been buried at the bottom of their lockers for most of the semester.

You are not in such great shape yourself. You've done a fair amount of studying, yet suddenly you can't remember what day it is, and you're not even sure where you are. The atmosphere seems more like that of a hospital emergency room than a classroom. Everyone in the room seems convinced that his life is on the line with this next big test.

This familiar scene is duplicated in classrooms across the country whenever a big test comes up. Just about every student has a stake in the results of a big exam. Even A+ students aren't immune to this test anxiety, since they want to secure their place at the top. The B and C students hope they can move up another grade notch. Even those students at the bottom hope they can pull themselves out of the hole by scoring well on a critical test.

Just what causes such universal anxiety? After all, tests measure only a small part of your learning. True. Yet test scores are the yardsticks by which teachers, admissions officers, and even some parents measure where you've been, where you are, and where you may be headed.

Many schools track students into various courses on the basis of test scores. Some parents peg allowances, bonuses, and privileges to good grades. Certainly college scholarships and admissions are connected to their applicants' test scores. Finally, there's you. Maybe you'll just *die* if you get anything less than a 90 on the next big test. If you're competitive and nothing less than a high grade will maintain your self-esteem, then it's no surprise that taking tests makes you nervous.

Reasons for test anxiety are as varied as the individual test-takers. Fortunately, the remedies are fairly simple. Test-taking is a skill like any other: it involves strategy, practice, a sense of confidence and, of course, basic knowledge of the class material. Study after study has shown that test-taking *skills* are as significant in raising scores as is the mastery of the basic material.

This means that if you and another person have exactly the same amount of knowledge, the person who is more skilled in test strategies will score higher, no matter what.

While this book doesn't provide the basic knowledge of subjects you can only get through your class work, it will show you how to develop skills, techniques, and shortcuts to help you make the most of what you *do* know.

PREPARING FOR TESTS

How do you develop test "wiseness"? Obviously all the skills in the world won't help you pass a test if you haven't cracked open a book or taken class notes all semester. Unfortunately, there's no substitute for long-term, day-to-day planning. But there are shortcuts you can follow to make the best use of your time and help you avoid those marathon study sessions.

Your test strategies should begin the first day of class and should become part of an ongoing study plan for each course. In the first few days of classes, most teachers give an overview of what they plan to cover in the course. Set aside a page in the looseleaf notebook to jot down some of the highlights of this overview.

Find out as much as you can about the test-maker, your teacher. Talk to students who have had the same teacher. Find out whether she encourages original thinking; such teachers are more likely to favor essay tests that require a lot of thinking and writing. Teachers who emphasize facts rather than the interpretation of those facts are likely to give objective tests and quizzes that require rote learning (repetition) or memorization.

See if you can get copies of your teacher's previous tests. A teacher's style, biases, and pet theories usually show up in the tests she designs. College students routinely keep files of old tests for review time; see if you can start a test file in your school. While you're not likely to get the exact test a student had the semester before, reviewing someone else's corrected exam gives you a sense of the *kind* of test your teacher is likely to give.

HOW TO LEARN MATERIAL FOR A TEST

For the anxious test-taker, the study scenario often goes like this: The teacher hands out a five-pound textbook the first day of class, along with a reading schedule of, say, five pages a night. The student starts out great guns. The first few nights, he's right on top of things; he even takes a quick glance at the study questions at the end of each chapter. If the teacher were to give a test at the end of the first week of class, this student would get an A+.

The daily diet of five pages is great—for a week. Then, a couple of weeks into the term, he slips behind a little. One night he's got band practice. Then he's out for a couple of days with the flu. Another time, he just can't work up enough steam to plow through the reading. It happens to nearly everyone.

Then about a third of the way into the semester, his teacher announces that in two weeks

4

she'll be giving a mid-term exam on all the class and textbook material. "Two weeks, no sweat," our intrepid scholar thinks. But somehow a week and a half goes by, and he discovers he's fifty pages in the hole with just a few days left before the mid-term.

At this point, the student sets out on a feverish course to cram weeks of reading into a couple of nights. He barely has time to flip though the pages, let alone coordinate his reading with his class notes. Everything is a big push to plow through those fifty pages and, if he's lucky, re-read the old material as well. He reads, reads, and reads more. Forget the class notes; there's no time. After all that frantic reading, is it any surprise that he can't remember his own name on the day of the test, let alone any of the textbook material he crammed into three nights?

You can see that a lot of energy was spent, or rather misspent, on this effort to cram a massive amount of reading into a short span of time. Moreover, this student bypassed a few other study methods that would have given him a better return on his investment of time and energy.

Let's take a look at a number of alternative ways any student might develop the kind of study skills that would pay off at test time—even allowing for band practice, sick days, and an occasional day off from studying.

Taking Class Notes

What's the next best thing to getting an advance copy of an upcoming test? Clues—the kind your teacher drops every time she says: "Most important," "Listen to this," "Above all," etc. Whenever your teacher repeats a fact, writes it on the board, or rephrases it in a new way, she's telling you the information is important.

At test time, well-organized class notes are your best study tool. The information in them is a guide to the material your teacher thinks is important enough to mention. Chances are, that same information will turn up on your tests as well.

Here's a plan for taking the kind of notes that will give you a boost on your tests:

1. Be prepared for class, so you can preview the main points of what the teacher will cover in class. Base your listening and note-taking on what you've already read.

2. Date your notes and leave some space between each day's entries so that you can go back and add more information if you need to later on.

3. Leave wide margins on each sheet for personal notes to yourself.

4. Record only main ideas. The purpose of note-taking is to help you focus on major points. To alert you to those points, here are some clues to listen for:

- *Openers:*

    "First . . ."

    "A major development . . ."

    "Take note of . . ."

    "The main theme is . . ."

    "The basic idea we're going to examine is . . ."

    "What's important to remember is . . ."

    "If you'll notice . . . you'll see that . . ."

- *Supporting Material:*
  "For example . . ."
  "For instance . . ."
  "Furthermore . . ."
  "As an example . . ."
  "Similarly . . ."
  "In contrast . . ."
  "On the other hand . . ."
  "Also . . ."

- *Conclusions:*
  "Finally . . ."
  "In summary . . ."
  "As a result . . ."
  "From this we can see . . ."
  "In conclusion . . ."

Write down any idea your teacher repeats more than once, and take notes on any material your teacher thinks is important enough to write on the board.

5. Summarize your teacher's remarks in the fewest possible words. Don't try to get every word down—just those that convey the idea. Explain ideas in your own words to help you think about what the statements really mean.

6. Arrange main ideas under headings. You can do this in outline form (see Appendix 4) or according to your own system. At review time, notes like this will tie together main ideas and the related supporting material.

7. If you have time, write down at least one example under your main headings. When you read your notes later on, one or two specific examples will refresh your memory of the main point.

8. Call attention to important words with symbols like stars, dots, exclamation points, question marks—anything that will help you notice information worth review before a test.

9. Use abbreviations wherever possible. Here are a few:

+	plus	∴	therefore
−	minus	w/	with
=	equal	w/o	without
ex. or e.g.	for example	info	information

10. Borrow notes for any class you missed. That might be the day your teacher decided to drop a lot of clues about an upcoming test.

Reading a Textbook

There's no good reason for ever reading all of your assigned textbook material more than once. The design of most textbooks provides you with excellent study tools: main headings, subheadings, review questions, etc. Those areas should be the focus of your review for any test.

Here are some shortcuts to help you tackle your textbook reading in the most efficient, helpful way possible:

1. Survey your textbook the first day you get it. Read the author's foreward or preface to see what the viewpoint is. Look at the table of contents to see how the book is organized and how much material is covered in the book. Scan the chapter headings and subheadings to see how the material is broken up. This quick survey, something you can do in fifteen minutes early in the course, provides you with an invaluable

overview of what your course is about. Everything you read after this quick survey will fit into the framework.

2. Before you do the detailed reading, survey each chapter as it is assigned. Skim the chapter title, headings, subheadings, and review questions to get a sense of what the chapter covers and how it is organized. This gives you a sense of where you're heading and how to get there.

3. Take note of any visual information—graphs, tables, diagrams, etc.—displayed in the chapters.

4. Pay special attention to words in bold type or italics; note topic sentences, summary paragraphs, or concluding sentences. At review time, these are the sections you should reread, not all the material.

5. Ask yourself questions as you read. What does the author mean? What are the author's biases? What key information is being presented?

6. Coordinate your class notes with the text material.

7. At test time, look at the book's table of contents, chapter headings, and subheadings. In your head, see if you can answer the questions at the end of the chapters. Instead of rereading all the material a second time, just concentrate on the book's summaries, important sections, opening and closing paragraphs in each chapter, and words that are in bold type or italics.

Making Up Outlines, Summaries, and Time Lines

When the pressure is on, it's tempting to revert to old study habits. Besides, who wants to add to the pile of materials that have to be reviewed? It's easier just to reread everything, right? Wrong. A few well-written study tools are far more effective in helping you retain information for a test. The process of making up a written outline, or summary is, in itself, a method of review. Don't you tend to remember things like phone numbers or grocery lists better when you've put them in writing? Here's how to make the most of your review time by making up written study tools.

Writing an Outline

An outline is a framework for organizing important ideas. The purpose of outlining is to cluster related pieces of information. During your review, concentrate on tying together main ideas and supporting facts; a short outline is the best way to do this. Here's a sample:

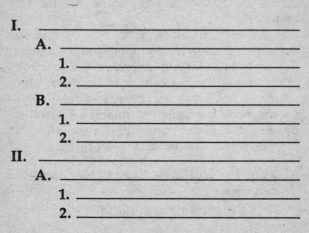

TOPIC: _____

I. _____

   A. _____

      1. _____

      2. _____

   B. _____

      1. _____

      2. _____

II. _____

   A. _____

      1. _____

      2. _____

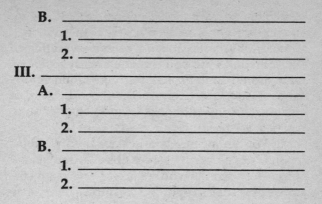

B. _____

   1. _____

   2. _____

III. _____

  A. _____

   1. _____

   2. _____

  B. _____

   1. _____

   2. _____

If you're outlining your textbook, the main headings go next to the Roman numerals, subheadings next to the letters, supporting facts next to the Arabic numerals.

If you have been taking class notes in outline form, then study from your notes. If not, make up an outline of your class notes by putting the most important ideas next to the Roman numerals, supporting points next to the letters, and related facts next to the Arabic numerals.

Writing a Summary

Summaries are for readers who want a quick overview of a subject without wading through a lot of facts and details. Many students find the process of writing a short summary is the best way to retain important information. A good summary helps the writer boil down material to its basics. Here's how to write a useful one:

1. Read material with the intention of summarizing it. This means being alert to main ideas and the way the author has organized them. The

best time to summarize your textbook assignments is right after you've read the material. Realistically, you probably won't be motivated to write one until you feel the pressure of a big test. Skim headings, subheadings, and opening and closing paragraphs; then condense that material. Many textbooks include chapter summaries; *use them.*

2. Put the information in your own words.

3. Write as briefly as possible. Group similar ideas. Join clauses with semicolons. Use only the most essential supporting examples to explain an idea.

4. Follow the same time structure as the original passage.

5. Keep in mind that a useful summary isn't a string of facts, but a miniature version of the highlights of the original material.

Writing a Time Line

A time line is a list of dates, events, or facts in chronological order. Instead of attempting to memorize random information, get yourself a long sheet of paper and simply list the important facts in a line moving down the page. Alongside your entries, write a phrase that explains each entry. A time line is one of the best ways to get a sense of the chronology and cause and effect of important events.

Reviewing for Tests

Reviewing is not an attempt to learn something for the first time, but a method of recalling and reinforcing previously learned material. Here's a systematic plan for getting the most out of your pre-test review:

1. A few weeks before the test, make sure you are caught up on all the assigned reading. Fill in any missing notes.

2. Go through your textbook and look at the headings and subheadings two or three times during the weeks before your test date. Write down page numbers of sections you're not sure about.

3. Take a few minutes several times during the weeks before the test to skim your notes.

4. A few days before your test, read the table of contents, the headings, and subheadings from your textbook. Make up an outline of these main ideas and see if you can fit a few supporting ideas and facts under each heading. You shouldn't have to spend more than fifteen minutes making up the outline.

5. On a second pass through your textbook, read the first and last paragraphs under each heading and subheading. Make sure you understand the main idea of each section you read. Look at the list of page numbers you made up for the sections you felt uncertain about. Read each of those listed pages or sections twice. If you're still having trouble with them, write a summary of what you think they mean.

6. Reread all your class notes *twice*. Read underlined or starred sections several times. If there are parts of your notes you don't understand, see if you can find something in your textbook that explains the confusion in a clearer way. Or see your teacher and have her help you out.

Memorization

Many students tend to think of memorizing

as a last-ditch attempt to stuff as much information as possible into their heads before a big test. Memorization, however, is more of a filing and retrieving skill that you can begin to develop the first day of class. It's a method of organizing information in a logical way, not simply the repetition of random facts.

Before you even try to memorize information for a test, keep the following in mind:

1. Select what you think is important to remember. From the first day of class, make a conscious effort to pull out only the most important information from your class notes and reading. Underline or star information your teacher keeps repeating; this is the kind of information worth remembering. Ideas, facts, and terms that appear over and over in your textbook also indicate the kinds of things you may have to remember.

2. Concentrate as you listen or read. Be an active reader and listener when you see or hear new information. Ask questions in class. Write things down. Discuss and criticize. Stay involved, and you'll give yourself more cues to help you retain information.

3. Rephrase new information in your own words. You can do this in your head or as part of a written summary.

4. Tie in new information with information you already know.

5. Read with a purpose in mind. As you go along, ask yourself what the main points are.

6. Organize information according to main and supporting ideas. Don't try to memorize anything without tying that information with another idea.

7. Repeat aloud what you are trying to memorize. A tape recorder can be a big help in memory work. Record what you are trying to learn into a tape, then keep playing it back. Or recite a term you want to memorize, leave a pause, then play back the tape and try to fill in the missing information. This is especially helpful when you are trying to memorize spelling and vocabulary words, or definitions for various subjects.

8. As you memorize, break down passages and paragraphs into sentences or single words.

9. Do your memory exercises in small blocks of time. Figure out your attention span, then only work for that amount of time on memorization.

10. Do your memory work a few days before the test date.

Predicting Test Questions

Anticipating what a test will cover is the best way to gear up for a big test. Look over old tests you have taken in that course or corrected exams from students who have had the same teacher in the past. Think about the kinds of questions your teacher asks in class discussions.

As you review material, see if there is some way it could be turned into a question. Here's how a statement from a history book might be turned into a test question:

Statement: "The rapid development of industry between 1865 and 1900 created many problems for wage earners in the United States. They attempted to solve some of the problems of working conditions, long hours, and low salaries by organizing labor unions."

Possible test questions: "What problems were created for workers during the rapid expansion of industry between 1865 and 1900?" or: "How did wage earners attempt to solve the problems brought about by the expansion of industry between 1865 and 1900?"

If you expect to get an essay test in a subject, formulate a few possible test questions (many textbooks have chapter-end questions) and do a mini-outline for each one to see if you can recall enough information to answer the question. On math and science tests, work out a few typical problems the night before to get yourself warmed up. Test yourself out loud in spelling, vocabulary, or grammar.

Forming a Study Group

In a study group, each member becomes an "expert" in one area of the course work, then shares his findings with other members who do the same thing. Get together with two or three studious classmates when the test date is announced. Sit down as a group and plan a schedule and strategy. Possible tasks include the preparation of individual summaries and the formulation of possible test questions. While all group members have to study all the material, individual members concentrate on a specific area. Each member should produce copies of notes on her area for everyone else in the group. A few nights before the test, the group meets to pool its collective information, predict questions, and test one another orally.

Cramming for a Test (If You've Been Ignoring All This Advice)

Cramming is a surefire way to lose your appetite, your sleep, and your self-respect. Having said that, cramming is an occasional fact of life for some students. Sometimes three mid-terms are scheduled on the same date; sometimes a whole semester slips by without your noticing it. Cramming does beat averaging a zero into the rest of your grade. If you can't reschedule a make-up test to give yourself breathing time to catch up, then cramming is your last resort.

The key to cramming effectively (keeping in mind that it's the least effective study method) is concentration. Here's how to do it if you have only one day left before a big test, you've only read half the material, and your notes are a mess, lost, or full of holes:

1. You're going to need a friend, preferably one who has kept up on the work. See if you can bribe that person to lend you her notes. Then

duplicate them on a copier at the library, return the notes, and vow eternal slavery for the favor.

2. Go through the copied notes. Underline, star, and highlight what you recall as being important in class. (This is assuming you attended all the classes.)

3. Then get out the textbook you've been avoiding all semester. Carefully read the table of contents, headings, subheadings, summaries, and review questions at least three times. If you have time, quickly skim the material. If there's no time, just stick to the boldface headings, opening and closing paragraphs, and any points which were also emphasized in class.

4. If you're being tested on math or science problems, pick out two or three typical examples and work them out as quickly as possible.

5. If you're being tested on rules, definitions, or spelling words, read each term or word silently five times, then aloud five times.

6. If you're being tested on novels and stories you've never read, you're in deep trouble. All you can do is reread your class notes, the book jackets, then try to get some sense of the book by reading the first and last chapters. Try to figure out the significance of any quotations or events you remember your teacher stressing in class.

7. Get some sleep. Researchers have found that concentrated study followed by a few hours of sleep works far better than a sleepless marathon of study up to test time.

THE COUNTDOWN BEFORE A BIG EXAM

The most nerve-wracking and least effective way to prepare for a test is the all-night, or even three-night, push to review everything. A more effective system is a step-by-step study effort that will actually take less time in the end.

Let's assume that your teacher gives you three weeks' notice for a major test. How can you best use that time to get ready? Here's one workable plan that allows for sufficient review and still gives you time to keep up on your soap operas and social life:

Three weeks before the test:

1. Write down the test date in your notebook and on your at-home calendar.
2. Ask your teacher these questions:
   - How much of the course material will be covered on the test? (There's no point in studying French grammar if your teacher only plans to include literature questions on the test.)
   - Will the test be an objective one (fill-in, true-false, multiple-choice, matching, etc.) or subjective (an essay test involving a lot of writing)? You'll see in the next few chapters that each type of test demands a special method of study and review.
   - How much of the exam counts toward your final grade?
3. Keep up on your class reading, noting main ideas. If you do get behind, set aside part of a weekend to catch up before the reading assignments get out of hand.

4. Maintain good class notes. Periodically skim your notes over the next three weeks to see if there are any unreadable or confusing sections. If you miss a class, borrow notes.

5. If you plan to use a study group, organize it early on.

6. Listen for hints about questions from your teacher. This is the time to star or check information she keeps stressing.

One to two weeks before the test:

1. Decide on your method of study. For an objective test, you'll want to emphasize memorization of facts; for an essay test, your grasp of large themes and ideas will be important.

2. Start rereading sections of your notebook you're not sure about. Ask questions in class about unclear information.

3. Make up any outlines, summaries, or time lines you plan to use. Make up lists of important points or areas that still stump you. Then work on mastering those sections.

4. Make up a list of possible test questions, and see if you can answer them in your head or in mini-outlines.

One or two nights before the test:

1. Start any memory work two nights before the test.

2. Get an overview in your mind. That way you'll have a framework in which to fit the particulars you are trying to commit to memory. To get this overview, once again, scan your notes, table of contents, headings, subheadings, summaries, and chapter-end questions. Review your study tools: outlines, summaries, lists, etc.

3. Reread any sections you still feel uncertain about.

4. Get your test equipment ready for class: two pens, two pencils, ruler, eraser, scratch paper, a watch, and anything else your teacher asked you to bring in on test day. Lay out your clothes, books, and notebook. Set your alarm extra early so that you don't start test day in a big, nervous rush.

Chapter 2

GENERAL TEST TACTICS

If you have ever wondered what specific skills and strategies separate confident A+ test-takers from those students who muddle through exams, take a look at the findings of a Cornell University researcher who asked 240 high-scoring students what their test secrets were. Here is how they ranked the importance of their test skills:

Read directions (or questions) carefully	44%
Don't spend too much time on one question	27%

*From the book, *The Complete Guide to Taking Tests: How to Earn Higher Scores on Any Exam with Test-Taking Strategies that Really Work*, by Bernard Feder. © 1979 by Bernard Feder. Published by Prentice-Hall, Inc., Englewood Cliffs, New Jersey 07632. Reproduced by permission.

Recheck your answers for errors	20%
Guess if you don't know the answers	18%
Eliminate possible foils and distractors	17%
Look for leads from other questions	13%
Answer easier questions first	8%
Plan your time	7%
Don't read into questions (or answers) too deeply	5%*

Let's assume you have revamped your study habits to help you prepare effectively for any kind of test. You have studied regularly, taken well-organized class notes, and conducted regular, short reviews of all your course material. This covers the knowledge end of your preparation. Now it's time to learn the ins and outs of dealing with the actual test.

Many poor test-takers waste valuable time and energy making decisions they should have made before going into the test — the kind of decisions that come automatically to students who score well on tests. Before you go into any test you should know what questions to ask your teacher; how to read directions; know whether or not to guess or change answers; whether to tackle hard or easy questions first; and how to work out a hard answer. Here are some answers to the kinds of questions you may be wondering about before a big test:

1. *What should you know before you actually start writing a test?* If the following information is not included in the test directions, find out from your teacher:

- the amount of time you have
- which questions are compulsory
- the point value of each question
- whether you will be penalized for wrong answers
- whether you can use scratch paper (Some teachers won't let you bring it into the test but will supply you with extra paper.)

2. *How should you read test directions?* Very carefully. Understanding test directions is the key to performing well on exams. A number of studies have shown that poor test-takers lose points because they misread directions or read them too quickly and miss key words.

Test directions contain valuable information about how you are to answer the questions. Certain key words make a difference in helping you spot right and wrong answers or in answering essay questions in a specified way. Here are some of the key words to look for and underline as you read exam directions:

fill in	underline
cross out	match
circle	
supply	

choose the best answer

choose the item that does not belong

answer yes or no

mark your answer with a
(check, letter, number)

complete all examples; or *x* examples

support your answers with
facts from the book

Read test directions at least twice, once for an overview of the requirements, a second time to underline key words.

3. *How should you plan your time?* Using the allotted test time efficiently is a key factor in scoring well on tests. Find out from your teacher or from the directions how much time you have for the whole test or any of its individual sections. On scratch paper or at the top corner of your test, divide the number of questions into the time you have (leaving five minutes for proofreading). For example, if you have to answer twenty questions worth the same number of points in roughly sixty minutes, you have a little less than three minutes to answer each one, allowing for the five minutes to proofread. Set aside more time for questions that are worth more points.

4. *Should you change answers?* Most test experts feel you should not change answers unless you are one hundred percent sure of your new information. Do consider changing an answer *if*:

- you realize you misread the question the first time around.
- you suddenly remember important, correct, new information.
- you come across key clues in another question.

Look over old tests you have taken. In the past, have you gained or lost points when you changed answers? Break the habit of changing answers if you have had a pattern of losing points. Finally, don't fritter away valuable test time wondering whether to change an answer unless you have a solid reason for doing do.

5. *Should you guess answers?* Yes, in most cases. Always guess answers on any test in which only right answers are counted. In other words, if your teacher is adding up points for correct answers rather than subtracting them for incorrect ones, then it pays to guess.

Before the test starts, find out if there's a penalty for guessing. If and when you do guess an answer, use logic, common sense, and clues from other questions to help you figure out the right answer on an objective test (fill-ins, true-false, matching, multiple-choice, etc.). If you have to guess an answer on an essay test, play up the ideas and facts you *do* know and avoid throwing around information you are not sure about.

6. *Should you answer easy or hard questions first?* Generally, answer easy questions before hard ones so that you can rack up points as quickly as possible, build your self-confidence, pick up clues to other questions, "warm up," or get insights to the hard questions, and get yourself into a working rhythm. However, it is more important to determine which questions are worth the most points. Then tackle the *easiest* of the *most valuable* questions first.

7. *What is the best way to tackle hard questions?* Save them for last (unless they are worth more), then:
- check key words in the question
- narrow your remaining options, eliminating obviously wrong choices
- break the question down into smaller parts
- rephrase the question in your own words

- see if you can find clues to the answer in other test items.

THE TEST SITUATION

You have been preparing fairly regularly for the big test, and now you have some preliminary "inside" information. On test day you are no longer among the bleary-eyed students staggering into the room. While you may have stayed up a little later than usual, you feel reasonably rested and just nervous enough to get the adrenaline going.

Once you get to your seat do a little slow, deep breathing. You may want to do a two-minute review of your study tools or read over the starred sections of your notes just to make sure you have the material tucked away. But don't attempt to cram information at this late date, and try not to get caught in the panicky conversations going on around you. After all, you are ready. If, despite all the groundwork you have completed, a moment of paralysis or blankness hits, doodle or write your name on the back page of the test sheet just to get your pen moving.

From the moment you have the test in hand, listen carefully to your teacher's comments. If you are unclear about anything, ask questions. Chances are other students are also confused about the same problems. Even after the test is underway, feel free to bring your paper up to the teacher and get any confusing questions cleared up.

Here are general test procedures to cover most kinds of tests:

1. Skim the entire test once to get a sense of what it covers.

2. Read the directions twice, underlining key words during your second reading. Determine the amount of time you have, the number of required questions, the scoring, and the form your answer should take.

3. Figure out a schedule by dividing the number of questions you have to answer into the number of minutes you have, devoting proportionately more time to valuable questions, and leaving five minutes for proofreading at the end of the test.

4. Tackle the easiest, most valuable required questions first. Put a check mark next to the hard questions you'll return to later.

5. As you work on each question, read it twice — first to get an overview, second to underline key words. Here is a list of key words:

> all
> always
> any
> best
> causes
> every
> exactly
> least likely
> most likely
> never
> not
> often
> only

opposite
probably
same as
unlikely

You'll find more key words listed in the chapters that deal specifically with various kinds of objective and essay tests.

6. Spend only the allotted time on each question unless you have time left over.

7. Once you have completed the questions you are sure about, attempt to answer the harder questions. Again, use only the allotted time to answer each item. *Do* guess answers to hard questions if you won't be penalized for doing so.

8. Keep working at maximum pace. Check your progress against the clock and against your schedule.

9. Proofread your test even if you haven't completed all the questions. Here's how:

- Reread the directions to make sure you complied with them throughout the test.
- Make sure you completed all the required questions.
- You may change an answer quickly if you are *very sure* of your new information.
- Mechanical errors can be very costly. They make your teacher's job harder. If you skipped a question, make sure you skipped a corresponding blank on your answer sheet.
- Check that spelling, grammar, punctuation, etc., are as correct as you can possibly make them. If you are not sure about

the spelling of a word, put "sp" in parentheses after the word to show you are aware of the possible error.

GENERAL TEST TIPS AND TRAPS

- Once you get the go-ahead on writing the test, write down any bits of information you're afraid of forgetting.
- Use all the time you have; you don't get extra points for finishing early and you may lose the goodwill of classmates who are still struggling through the material.
- Read every word in the question; don't jump to conclusions.
- Completely cross out or erase answers so that you are not penalized.
- Use clues in easy questions to answer hard ones.
- Ask for an explanation of confusing questions or directions.
- Rephrase tricky questions.
- Try for partial credit if only right answers are being counted.
- Make the most of what you *do* know; avoid what you obviously know nothing about.
- Above all, start a test file. This is important. An old test is a useful study tool for a later test. Where did you gain or lose points? What are your good and bad habits? What is the teacher's test style? What does he like to see in a test? These ques-

tions can only be answered by keeping track of corrected tests. While it may be tempting to throw away a test marked with a 60, a test on which you did poorly is valuable in showing you what to avoid next time around.

Chapter 3

HOW TO TAKE OBJECTIVE TESTS

Most students prefer taking objective tests rather than essay exams. An objective test asks you to supply, recall, fill in, choose, or match up short, factual answers. This kind of test requires a minimum of writing and offers more possibilities for guessing answers — two good reasons why they are popular with students. Teachers tend to favor objective tests because they are easier to design and grade.

The objective test appears in four basic forms: true-false; multiple choice; matching; and fill-in; each of which is discussed in detail later in this chapter.

GENERAL PREPARATION FOR OBJECTIVE TESTS

Because objective tests demand the recall of facts, dates, rules, formulas, definitions, names, statistics, and so forth, memory work is particularly important at test time. As you take class notes, read and review your textbook and underline, star, or list important factual information your teacher keeps stressing. Try to tie each item to main ideas and themes as you take note of them.

Of course, you can't possibly memorize all the facts that come up in your course. How do you decide which facts are worth memorizing? First think about the important themes, ideas, and theories mentioned in class and in your text. Then look for related facts and details that back up those "big ideas." For example, if the theme of rebellion has been stressed in your American history class and textbook, review the names, dates, incidents, and locations connected with acts of rebellion during the period you are studying. If you are learning about osmosis in biology, write down the facts connected with that process.

Memorizing isolated facts won't help you on an objective test; connecting related facts and details with larger ideas is a more effective way to prepare for this kind of test. "Buzz words" from your courses like "rebellion" or "osmosis," for example, will trigger off related information if you made the necessary connections as you reviewed and memorized for the test.

ANSWERING THE HARD QUESTIONS ON OBJECTIVE TESTS

All objective tests have certain things in common: language, choices, certain pitfalls. Here is some inside information to help you plan your strategy for dealing with the demands of this kind of test:

- See if you can think of the answer to an objective question in your head before you look at the answer choices. As soon as you spot the same answer among the possibilities, write it down, then move on to the next question.
- Eliminate obviously wrong choices by crossing them out. This narrows your options.
- Rephrase confusing questions in your own words.
- Read the "stem" of the question with each of the likely choices if you get stuck. (The stem is the first part of the question that has to be completed with one of the possible choices.) This way you can spot inconsistencies in language, pluralization, grammar, subject-verb agreement, etc. This process also gives you a sense of how the whole items "sound" to you.
- See if there are clues to hard questions in any of the other items.
- Underline key words in objective tests. Here is a list of them, arranged in related groups:

all	always	equal	good
every	invariably	less	best
many	sometimes	more	bad
most	seldom		worst
few	usually		
some	never		
none			

TYPES OF OBJECTIVE TESTS

There are four basic knds of objective tests teachers give: true-false, multiple-choice, matching, and fill-in. For the most part, the right answer is listed among a choice of answers for each of these types of tests. Your job is to find it. Many teachers give combination tests, that is, a mix of some of the four types, or in addition to one or two essay questions. In planning your test strategy, determine which section is worth the most points and work on that first. If, for example, the essay questions are worth seventy-five points out of a hundred and the multiple choice section is worth only twenty-five points, spend seventy-five per cent of your time on the essay questions and twenty-five on the multiple-choice section.

True-False Tests

The true-false test asks you to verify whether a statement is right or wrong. Since you only have two choices per question, this seems like a relatively easy kind of test. To make such tests more challenging, teachers usually give you a limited amount of time to work on a huge number of true-false items. Further, the presence or absence of a single word can make this kind of test tricky indeed.

Preparation

Review facts, dates, rules, formulas, names, and statements stressed in your text and in class. Memorize and connect these bits of information to the main ideas in your course, which are likely to reappear as part of true-false statements. One useful study tool for this kind of test is a two-column list showing main ideas on one side and a few facts on the other. For example:

osmosis:
semipermeable membrane
solvent
solution
cells

Teachers often pull out true statements right from the textbook or class lectures so, as you study, pay special attention to important ideas.

Test Tactics

1. Read the directions twice, underlining important words. Determine whether you are supposed to check off the true statements or the false ones, or whether you are to mark the questions with a "T" or an "F." From the directions, figure out how much time you have for the true-false section and divide the number of minutes you have by the number of items you have to answer. Leave five minutes for proofreading.

2. If there is time, skim all the questions. Chances are, though, that you won't have time to skim the entire test.

3. Tackle the easy questions first, since building up points quickly is important on a true-false test. Put a check next to those you're not sure about. You can return to them later if there is time.

4. Read each choice quickly but carefully, paying attention to the key words mentioned earlier in this chapter.

5. If an answer pops into your head right after you have read the question carefully, write it down. Don't waste time pondering your choice on this kind of test unless you have time left over later on.

6. On a second pass, attempt to answer the questions you skipped. Don't spend too much time on any individual item since they are all worth the same number of points. If you won't be penalized for incorrect answers, take a guess at the hard questions. One word of caution. Since it's so easy to guess on this type of test because you have a fifty-fifty chance of being right, this is one of the rare times that teachers penalize you for guessing by subtracting points for wrong answers. If wrong answers are scored this way, do only shrewd guessing.

7. Proofread your test by rereading the directions, making sure you answered the required items and trying to reason out answers to the hard questions.

Tips and Traps on True-False Tests

- If any part of a true-false statement is false — even a single word — the entire statement is false.

- Restrictive words — *all, always, none, never, only, every, invariably, sole, absolutely* — usually make a statement false since they limit the statement so much.
- Qualifiers that make a statement more believable usually appear in true statements. They include:

after	greatest	often
average	in general	or
best	last	partially
but	later	partly
chiefly	least	perhaps
could	lowest	probably
easiest	mainly	rarely
eventually	maximum	seldom
except	minimum	smallest
frequently	more	sometimes
generally	most	usually

- The word *not* is a booby trap that can mislead a careless or unwary test-taker. Watch out for it.
- On this kind of test, there are usually more true than false statements because it's easier to write a true statement right from the textbook than to create a believable false one.

Multiple-choice Tests

The multiple-choice test is a variation of the true-false objective test, only it contains more choices. On this kind of test, you are asked to select a single answer from several possibilities.

Example:
How many states ratified the Constitution?
a. 9
b. 11
c. 13
d. 6

Preparation

Again, try to connect facts, phrases, dates, statistics, definitions, etc., with the main themes and terms you have been studying. Pre-test yourself by reciting or writing key words, then seeing how many related facts or phrases you can associate with each one.

Test Tactics

1. Skim the entire test once to get a sense of what it's about.

2. Read the directions twice, underlining key words. From the directions, determine how much time you have, how much the questions are worth, and how many questions are compulsory. Note whether you are to choose the correct, incorrect, or best answer, or the answer that belongs or does not belong in a group with the other choices.

3. Read each question twice, underlining key words as you do.

4. Answer easy questions first and mark the hard ones so that you can return to them later on.

5. Understand what is actually being asked, not what you think is being asked.

6. Rephrase the question in your own words

if you don't understand it.

7. Proofread your paper by rereading the directions, making sure you answered the compulsory items and trying to figure out the hard questions you checked off.

Tips and Traps on Multiple-choice Tests

- Broad or absolute statements like *all, none, always, never, forever,* or *totally* <u>seldom</u> appear in <u>correct</u> answers.
- Qualifying words like *generally, often, frequently, usually, seldom,* or *sometimes,* <u>frequently</u> appear in <u>correct</u> answers.
- Eliminate obviously incorrect choices to narrow down the correct possibilities.
- Be alert for wording that looks and sounds familiar, since teachers often pull a correct statement from the textbook or class lectures.
- Watch for the booby trap, *not,* which can trip you up on a multiple-choice test.
- When you tackle hard questions, read the stem along with each of the choices so that you can spot consistencies or inconsistencies in grammar, punctuation, subject-verb agreement, and agreement of *a/an* with vowels and consonants.
- Look for context clues within the question. For example, in a question asked about a French leader, you could narrow your choices by looking at French-sounding names.
- Look for clues to one question in other questions.

Matching Tests

Matching tests ask you to associate related ideas, terms, statements, etc., which appear in columns. To make the test more challenging, some teachers throw in extra choices in one of the columns.

Preparation

You can pre-test yourself for a matching test by listing one column of important terms, ideas, statements, etc., then writing down as many related facts as you can associate with each of the entries. Then use this pre-test as your study tool. Again, it is important to learn the material in clusters, associating related information with larger ideas.

Test Tactics

1. Skim both columns before you start writing, so that you can consider all the possible combinations.

2. Read the directions twice, underlining key words as you go along.

3. Schedule your time by dividing the number of minutes you have by the number of questions on the test.

4. Work your way down the column with the fewest items. That way you won't get distracted by the "extra" choices if there are any. If both columns have the same number of entries, work from the column with the most words in each item. These longer phrases provide more clues. You'll also save time this way, since you will only be rereading the shorter choices as you go along.

5. Do the easy items first, crossing out choices as you run through the questions. This narrows down the items that may cause you difficulty.

Tips and Traps on Matching Tests

- Match like with like; that is, items that obviously go together, e.g., names with achievements, actions, discoveries, inventions; locations and the events that happened there; dates with events or birthdays; institutions with their functions; laws and rules with their dates or founders.
- Only work down one column at a time; switching back and forth is confusing and time-consuming.
- Unless you are instructed to do so, don't draw lines to connect items.
- Cross out each match as you find it.

Fill-In Tests

The fill-in test asks you to complete a statement with a logical word or phrase. Like the multiple-choice test, it may contain a stem that you have to complete. Or you may have to complete the statement with a word or phrase within the statement.

Preparation

Teachers often pull out sentences from the textbook or class lectures to use in fill-in tests, so study the statements that have been stressed in class. Again associate key words, phrases, facts, and details with larger main ideas. That way, the mention of one of those ideas will trigger off related material.

Test Tactics

1. Skim the entire test.
2. Read the directions twice, underlining key words.
3. Schedule your time by dividing the number of minutes you have by the number of questions you have to answer. Leave a few minutes for proofreading.
4. Read each question twice before you attempt to answer it. Underline key facts in the questions. See if you can think of the answer first before you actually check the possible answers. If you spot it among the choices, write down the answer.
5. Cross out each choice as you go along.
6. Complete the easy questions first, marking the hard ones so that you can return to them later.
7. Proofread your paper by rereading the directions, making sure you answered the required number of questions and answering the hard questions you skipped.

Tips and Traps for Fill-in Tests

- Look for grammatical clues, subject-verb agreement, punctuation, *a/an* agreement, and consistent language to help you figure out hard fill-in questions.
- Use the number of blanks or the length of them as clues. Most teachers are on to

this gimmick, so they usually provide the same size blanks for all the questions, but if not, this is a tactic worth trying if you are really stuck for an answer.

- If choices are not provided and you don't know what to fill in, take a guess if you won't be penalized. You may be able to get partial credit for a nearly right answer.

Chapter 4

HOW TO TAKE LONG AND SHORT ESSAY TESTS

The announcement of an essay test often elicits a wave of groans from many students who dread writing under any conditions, let alone within the brief time limits of an essay exam. While there is some comfort in knowing that you have to master facts for objective tests, you may be confused about preparing for essay exams.

From the teacher's viewpoint, essay tests present problems as well. The prospect of correcting endless and varied responses to open-ended questions is almost enough to make many teachers revert to the simple true-false test. Yet teachers usually include essay questions on important exams because such items challenge students' thinking and creativity. Essay tests measure your grasp of ideas and your ability to develop them logically.

For these reasons, essay tests are a fact of life

in many classes. Since this kind of test is worth more on your final grade, it is worth learning how you can score well on them.

LONG ESSAY TESTS

Preparation

Your teacher's interpretation of your ideas on an essay test is the major factor in your grade. Therefore, it is critical to understand your teacher's biases, pet theories, and arguments when you get ready for an essay exam. What ideas keep cropping up in class? Which side does your teacher take on various issues? If you take an opposite position, can you defend your views with proof from your reading?

Cramming before an essay exam is futile. This kind of test demands an understanding of the major highlights of your course backed up by specific evidence — the kind of information that is difficult to master in an "all-nighter." If you find that you have missed a lot of the assigned reading, your only recourse is to read chapter summaries and the important sections of your notes and hope that you can stretch out this skimpy knowledge.

When your teacher announces the next essay exam, find out which major themes you are expected to review. Most teachers are fairly open about reviewing the main themes before a big test of this kind.

Look at the table of contents, headings, and subheadings of your text as well as any chapter summaries it might include. Get a good overview of the development and chronology of important ideas in the book. Use your notes as a guide for reviewing sections of material your teacher is likely to include on the test.

A few weeks before the exam, prepare a study sheet or outline. This should include a list of all the major ideas your teacher has covered in class and assigned in the reading. Following is part of a study outline for a history essay test. Notice how related facts, details, and names support and develop each main theme. At test time, this kind of supporting information can make the difference between a rambling essay answer and one that is focused and well developed.

OUTLINE: American History Exam

I. Spirit of Compromise at Constitutional Convention (1787)
    A. Delegates were a cross-section
       1. Some signed Declaration of Independence; others diplomats
          a. Benjamin Franklin
          b. Madison, A. Hamilton
    B. Areas of Agreement
       1. Believed new Constitution was needed
       2. Country needed a strong central government
       3. No section of government could dominate the others; executive, legislative, and judicial powers separated
       4. Government must have power to tax
    C. Disagreements
       1. Economics
       2. Regional differences; large vs. small states

II. The Great Compromise — Roger Sherman (Connecticut)
   A. Population of states to determine representatives to House
      1. Virginia Plan
      2. New Jersey Plan
   B. Each state would have two senators

Test Tactics: Long Essay Tests

The day a teacher hands back corrected essay tests is one filled with questions, comments, comparisons, and complaints: "I wrote twice as much as so and so, and all I got was a B– and she got an A"; "I think I deserve five more points because I mentioned such and such"; or "How come I lost three points on the third question?"

Although subject to both the test-taker's and the grader's interpretation, successful essay tests share certain characteristics. Knowing what these qualities are can help you earn the maximum number of points for developing what you know. Here are several tried and true characteristics that you would find on most well-written essay exams:

- The writer answers all parts of the actual question.
- The writer states the main idea immediately. No teacher correcting a mountain of tests wants to read through half the answer to find the main point.
- Each paragraph of the essay expands and develops a single aspect of the main point.
- The writer backs up the main point and each supporting idea with proof in the form of facts, details, examples, data,

quotations, reasons, definitions, etc.

- The writer presents information in logical order.
- The writer provides the teacher with connecting or transitional words that guide the reader from one point to the next in an organized way. These connectives include, by category, the following:

CONNECTIVES THAT INDICATE A SEQUENCE

and, additionally, in addition, also, furthermore, another, moreover, likewise, similarly, next, finally, besides, again, first, secondly, in conclusion, in summary

CONNECTIVES THAT INDICATE A TIME OR SPATIAL RELATIONSHIP

soon, next, then, later, finally, eventually, first, second, etc., now, meanwhile, in the meantime, afterward, since, nearby, above, below, beyond, in front, in back

CONNECTIVES TO INDICATE CONTRAST

but, on the other hand, however, rather, nevertheless, otherwise, yet, still, in spite of

CONNECTIVES TO INDICATE RESULTS

therefore, hence, because, thus, consequently, as a result, for, accordingly, so

CONNECTIVES USED TO INDICATE EXAMPLES

for example, for instance, in other words, in the case of

- The writer sums up the main point in a

concluding sentence or short paragraph that leaves the teacher with a clear impression of the test-taker's point of view.
- The essay answer is neat, readable, and grammatically correct.

Organization and efficient use of time are the keys to scoring well on an essay test. On exam day, follow these steps when you get the question sheet:

1. Scan the entire exam to get a sense of what it covers.

2. Determine from your teacher or from the directions the number of questions you are required to answer, the amount of time you have for the whole test and for each question, the point value of each question, the style or method by which you are to answer the questions (with a pen? on alternate pages? every other line?), and whether or not you can use scratch paper or write notes on the back of the test sheet or booklet for reference.

3. Once you have scanned the test, write down any factual information you don't want to forget. Use your scratch paper for this purpose.

4. Plan a schedule by dividing the number of minutes you have by the number of questions you have to answer, devoting proportionately more time for more valuable questions and five minutes for proofreading at the end.

5. Decide which of the compulsory questions you will answer. Do the most valuable, easiest questions first.

6. Read the question twice, noting these important key words:

Analyze: Examine the subject in question by discussing its parts.

Comment: State your own views about the subject by explaining, criticizing, or illustrating its meaning.

Compare: Examine two things and show, with examples, how they are alike.

Contrast: Examine two things and use examples to point out their differences.

Compare and Contrast: This is a combination of the two previous items.

Criticize: Give your judgment or opinion about the subject of the question. Show its good and bad points.

Define: Tell what the statement or subject in the question means.

Demonstrate: Use examples to provide or explain the subject.

Describe: Present a detailed account in a logical sequence.

Develop: Follow a logical path that leads from the first point about a subject to its concluding points.

Diagram: Use charts, graphs, drawings, and labels to illustrate an aspect of the subject of the question.

Discuss: Examine and analyze in detail the significance of the subject of the question. Offer pros and cons.

Enumerate: Name, list, and number main ideas one by one.

Evaluate: Give your opinion (or an expert's opinion) of the value of an idea. Point out its advantages and disadvantages.

Explain: Give reasons for or causes of something.

Illustrate: Explain or clarify an idea or theme by using specific examples, comparisons, or analogies.

Interpret: Explain the meaning of something.

Justify: State why you think something is the way it is. Give reasons for your views.

Outline: Present the structure of a theme or idea in categories.

Prove: Show by argument or logic that something is true.

Relate: Show how things are connected.

Review: Make a general survey of the subject; it may also mean to criticize a subject. Clear this up with your teacher.

State: Present main points in brief, clear sentences.

Summarize: Give a brief chronological acount of main ideas.

Trace: Follow the progress, historical events, or development of the subject in question.

7. Don't begin answering the question until you have read it twice and made up a mini-outline or list of points and details you plan to include in your answer. This process is a real timesaver because it gives you a chance to list everything you know about the question. You can then develop your knowledge without starting and stopping as things pop into your head. The few minutes this step takes will save you many minutes on your test schedule.

On your mini-outline or list, write down the main idea you want to present, a few important points that develop the main idea, and supporting details that provide evidence for your views. Put this information in chronological order in an outline or number each point in the order in which you plan to use them. Here's an example:

Question: Describe the Lincoln-Douglas Debates.

OUTLINE:

Main point: Lincoln-Douglas debates (1858) helped A.L. move into national spotlight.

I. Background
   A. Lincoln confident of views
      1. Forced Douglas to take an unpopular position
         a. D. for slavery
         b. Debates in an anti-slavery state, Illinois
      2. "House divided" quote
   B. Douglas in defensive position
      1. Dred Scott decision — went against
      2. Freeport Doctrine was D.'s defense

II. Results
   A. Douglas won Illinois but lost Southern supporters
   B. Lincoln got national publicity for future Presidential election

8. Using your mini-outline or list as your reference, write your answer. State your main idea clearly in the first sentence so that your teacher knows exactly where you stand. Expand this idea with supporting points and facts from your

list or outline. Cross off those entries as you use them. Use connectives to tie your ideas and details together. Summarize your main idea in the last sentence. As soon as you have covered all parts of the question, move on to the next one. Stick to your initial schedule for each question.

9. Proofread your answers. Check that:
- you have answered all parts of the question.
- you have fulfilled all the requirements of the directions by rereading them.
- you haven't left out important words and phrases.
- your answers are neat, readable, and correct in matters of grammar, punctuation, and spelling.

Tips and Traps on Long Essay Tests:

- Keep your teacher in mind as you write. Make her job as easy as possible so that she'll look at your paper favorably and give you the benefit of the doubt on answers that are a bit off the point or slightly incomplete.
- Watch out for multi-part questions. Here's an example: "What did King James I promise in the 1606 charter? Why was this promise important to the colonists? Explain." In multi-part questions underline the key topic words, in this case, "What," "Why," and "Explain."
- Focus on opening and closing sentences since these make the first and most lasting impressions. Answer the question in the first sentence and wrap up the answer in the last sentence.

- Adopt a definite and authoritative point of view from the beginning and stick with it.
- Be convincing. Use positive words and phrases along with active verbs. Avoid the passive voice and fuzzy statements like: "I think"; "Maybe"; "It seems." Rather than begin: "I feel Lincoln launched his Presidential career in his debates with Douglas," say: "Lincoln launched his . . ."
- Sprinkle your essay answers with key words, phrases, terms, and statements your teacher has used in class. Teachers are pleased when students actually remember verbatim statements.
- Cite authorities by quoting or paraphrasing them. You could build almost any kind of essay answer about Lincoln by using his quotation: "A house divided against itself cannot stand." Direct or even partial quotations are impressive and lend a note of authority to your answer.
- If you run short of time, cut back on the number of supporting details you write, not main ideas.
- In a pinch, make the most of what you do know so that you can get at least partial credit for an answer. Avoid throwing in details about which you are unclear. This tips off your teacher that you are faking your way through an answer.
- If you aren't sure about how to state a main point, raise your own question and

answer it. For example, if you wanted to discuss the Dred Scott decision in an essay question about the Lincoln-Douglas debates, you could bring up the subject by asking in your essay: "Why did Lincoln repeatedly ask Douglas to explain his views about the Dred Scott decision?" Then you could proceed to answer the question. This kind of thinking shows initiative.

- Use a good pen; penciled papers get blurred too easily. If you have to cross out words, do so neatly and completely.
- Write on one side of that paper so that your writing is more readable. Consider skipping lines in case you want to add information later on.
- Save all your old essay tests to get a sense of your strengths and weaknesses. Swap papers with another student when you get them back to see if there's a system to your teacher's grading. Are there areas where you or a classmate lost or gained points? Take note of them for the next essay test.

THE SHORT ESSAY TEST

The short essay test is a cross between an objective test and a long essay exam and can be trickier than either one. In this kind of test, you have to supply facts rather than choose them as you would in an objective test, yet you have far less time than you would have in an essay exam to develop those facts.

Preparation

The most common short essay question asks you to define a particular term or identify the significance of a person, place, event, or date. To study for this kind of test, make a list of the main ideas from your course and the important facts that relate to those ideas. One effective way to do this is to read off your list into a tape recorder or have a friend say each item aloud. In either case, you then rattle off as many associated details as you can within a minute or so. Don't concern yourself with reciting or writing whole sentences at study time; what's important is the clustering of ideas around the main themes you have covered in class and in your reading.

Test Tactics: Short Essay Tests

If you have studied the class material, and you know how to write a concise paragraph, then you're in good shape for the short essay test. Let's examine the characteristics of a well-organized and developed paragraph.

- A topic sentence states the main idea. In a short essay test, this is where you answer the main part of the question.
- The paragraph develops the topic sentence.
- Supporting sentences illustrate or prove the validity of the main idea through examples, facts, reasons, anecdotes, definition, comparisons, and quotations.
- All sentences relate directly to the topic sentence.

Here are the steps involved in answering questions on a short essay test:

1. Scan the test once to see what it covers.

2. From your teacher or from the directions, determine how many questions you have to answer; how much time you have to answer them; how much each question is worth; what minimum number of facts you must include in each answer; and whether or not you can use scratch paper or make notes.

3. Jot down facts and details you want to remember on your scratch paper or the back of the test sheet.

4. Read the directions twice, underlining key words. (These are mentioned earlier in this chapter.)

5. Schedule your time by dividing the number of minutes you have by the number of required questions. Leave five minutes for proofreading.

6. Answer the easiest, most valuable questions first.

7. Read each question twice, underlining key words. Then, on scratch paper, write down in a phrase the main idea. Alongside that main idea, list three or four related facts. Either put this information in an outline or number each item in the order in which you plan to use them. With your outline or list before you, write a clear topic sentence that answers the question right off the bat. Then support this topic sentence with your facts and details. Make sure you only make one main point. Stick to your schedule.

8. Tackle the hard questions once you have completed the easy ones. Try for partial credit if you won't be penalized for doing so. Teachers

often give a point for each correct fact mentioned, so if you know just one or two, see if you can form some kind of topic sentence that you can develop partially with those two facts.

9. Proofread your test by rereading the directions and making sure you have complied with them; by checking that you have answered all possible questions; and by making certain grammar, punctuation, spelling, and legibility are in order.

Tips and Traps on Short Essay Tests

- Come right to the point.
- Here's a formula for answering most short essay questions:
    - Fit the item into a category.
    - Date the item.
    - Place it in a specific location.
    - Give a reason why the item is important.
    - Associate a name with the item.
    - Emphasize the facts you do know. Try not to pad a short essay answer, because it's so easy for teachers to spot incorrect information.

Chapter 5

HOW TO TAKE TESTS IN DIFFERENT SUBJECT AREAS

Are you a whiz in English but tongue-tied when it comes to a foreign language? Does your mind work like a computer in math but grind to a halt in history? If so, you are like many students who breeze through tests in certain subjects but have to struggle for every point in others.

Each of your subjects has its own vocabulary, organization, and viewpoint, all of which demand special approaches. Memorizing the steps of a geometry formula is different from remembering how to say: "Where is the pencil?" in French. Here is a rundown of special information to help you deal effectively with the individual requirements of tests in different subjects.

VOCABULARY TESTS

Preparation

Don't wait until just before the test to start memorizing the definitions of assigned words. As soon as you get a new word in class, start using it right away in your speech and writing. If you do this conscientiously, you can cut your study time for vocabulary tests considerably.

There will always be some words that stump you. Follow this procedure as close as possible to the test date: Read the word and its definition aloud five times, write the word and its meaning five times, then use it in a sentence.

The night before a vocabulary test, corral a willing friend, family member (or a tape recorder), and have him/her/it recite your list of assigned words one by one as you say the definition. If you use a tape recorder, play back the tape a few times after you have done your recitation so that you can "hear" the meanings in your head.

Tactics, Tips, and Traps

- Know these key words before you go into any vocabulary test: *synonyms* (words that have nearly the same meaning); *antonyms* (words that have opposite meanings); *homonyms* (words that look and sound similar, but have different meanings, e.g., *bear*, to carry, and *bear*, an animal); *homophones* (words pronounced like each other, but with different meanings and spellings, e.g., *to*, *two*, *too*).

- Be alert to these tricky phrases in vocabulary test directions and questions: "Choose the word that: *does not belong; is opposite in meaning to . . .;* or *is the same as . . ."*
- Use context clues (other words in the question) to help you figure out the meaning of a word.
- In a multiple-choice vocabulary test, see if you can define the word in your head before you look at the choices. If you spot it among the possibilities, write your answer and move on quickly to the next question.
- Use prefixes, suffixes, and root words as clues to figure out the meanings of words. You'll find a list of these word parts in your grammar book. If, for example, you know that the prefix *inter* means *between*, you might be able to guess that the meaning of *intercede* is *to come between*.

GRAMMAR TESTS

Preparation

Reread and memorize the assigned grammar rules a few nights before the test. Read each one five times. Say it aloud five times, and write it down once. Write an example of the rule in a sentence. Skim through all the grammar exercises you were assigned in class. Teachers often pick the same or similar examples from previously assigned exercises. Do at least two examples from each exercise. Look over old homework sheets. Where did you have problems? Work on those examples again.

Tactics, Tips, and Traps

- As you study and memorize grammar, group related rules; that is, study pronoun rules as a group; agreement rules together, etc.
- Grammar and punctuation fall under six main rules: sentence rules; subject-verb agreement; verb tenses; style and construction; punctuation; pronoun agreement.

SPELLING TESTS

Preparation

Learn spelling words as they are assigned, and use them in your speech and writing. Keep up a list of spelling demons in your notebook — words that trip you up every time, words you get wrong on quizzes. This process provides you with a good study tool for mid-term and final exams.

When you memorize spelling words, break each word into syllables to make your job easier. If you are not sure where to divide the syllables, use a dictionary to look up the word. In fact, if you really want to become a good speller, keep a pocket dictionary handy. Checking a word's spelling is one of the best ways to remember it.

The night before your exam, pre-test yourself by using a tape recorder or having a friend recite the word as you spell it aloud or in writing.

Tactics, Tips, and Traps

- Alphabetize your list of assigned spelling words before you memorize them, or group words that have similar spellings and study them that way.
- Relate new spelling words to easier ones you already know.
- Learn how basic root words, prefixes, and suffixes are spelled. You'll find these word parts listed in any good grammar book. Taking the time to familiarize yourself with these parts helps you in both spelling and vocabulary.
- Here are some rules and memory devices to help you develop effective spelling techniques:

  1. Drop the final *e* before a suffix that begins with a vowel. Examples: *bake + ing = baking; love + able = lovable.* Exceptions: If the *e* is preceded by a soft *c* or *g* sound, keep the final *e*. Examples: *notice + able = noticeable; change + able = changeable.*

  2. When the suffixes *ness* and *ly* are added, the root word remains the same. Examples: *kind + ness = kindness; usual + ly = usually.*

  3. When the prefixes, *dis, il, im, in, mis, over, re,* and *un* are added, the root word remains the same. Examples: *dis + arm = disarm; il + legible = illegible; im + possible = impossible, in + active = inactive; mis + behave = misbehave; over + board = overboard; re + do = redo; un + mistakable = unmistakable.*

4. When the vowel sound in a word is *ee*, the *i* follows the *e* except after *c*. Examples: *achieve, belief, reprieve* (but *receive*).

5. When the vowel sound is not pronounced *ee*, the spelling is *ei*. Examples: *foreign, veil, freight, weight* (the exceptions are *friend, handkerchief, sieve*).

LITERATURE TESTS

Preparation

As you read assigned novels, plays, and poems, list the page numbers of important passages and quotations. Then at review time, all you have to do is go back and read over those pages as well as any others that were stressed in class. To refresh your memory of a book for a test, reread the preface, author's notes, jacket copy, and the first and last chapters of the book, or the first and last five pages.

Ask yourself some of the following questions as you read.

1. What is the main idea of the work?

2. What is the conflict?

3. How are the characters affected by the events that happen in the book?

4. Are main ideas presented through the author's narrative voice or through one of the characters?

5. What is the author's purpose?

6. How significant is the setting to the book?

7. Are the characters well developed?

8. What experiences or character traits are like your own?

These are the kinds of essay questions many English teachers ask in literature tests, so get in the habit of asking them yourself, and you'll be in good shape at test time.

Tactics, Tips, and Traps

- Use a folded notebook page as a bookmark when you first read an assigned book. Keep track of page numbers, passages, quotations, and questions you have as you read along. When you finish the book, put the bookmark-page back in your notebook and use it as a study aid before a test.
- Memorize at least two significant quotations from the assigned material. Make sure they reflect the spirit and theme of the book. Use the quotation within an appropriate answer somewhere in your test paper, and you're bound to gain a lot of points for doing so.

MATHEMATICS TESTS

Preparation

Memorize math formulas and math vocabulary: formulas to cover the numerical parts; and definitions like *area*, *volume*, *perimeter*, *tangent*, etc., to master the vocabulary sections. Keep a math "dictionary" in your notebook for new terms. Jot down illustrations or examples of the term or rule next to each entry. The night before a math test, work out at last two examples of each kind of assigned problem from the class.

Tactics, Tips, and Traps

- When you do homework problems in math throughout the semester, work out at least one problem under "test" conditions, i.e., within a short time limit to see how well you can follow steps under pressure. This is an excellent warm-up for any math quiz or exam.
- Copy down formulas exactly, and next to each one write your own personal notes for working it out. Use these notes as study sheets at test time.
- If you find your math book too difficult, see if you can find an easier one.
- Do practice problems as soon as they come up in class so that all the steps are fresh in your mind.
- Almost more than any other subject, math concepts build from the previous steps. If you miss a class or misunderstand something, catch up or clear up any confusion immediately.
- Use shortcuts as you work out problems on a test. Estimate, cancel fractions, remove decimal points, etc.
- Mathematical problems are composed of several parts. After you read the question at least three times, underline, circle, or number each section you will have to answer.

SCIENCE TESTS

Preparation

Science is a subject based on a network of

systems and classifications, so it's important to review terms, formulas, and data within the framework of science. At the beginning of the year, look over the table of contents, headings, and subheadings to get a sense of the organization of the subject. Keep this overview in mind as you read and review the particulars.

Start a science "dictionary" in a special section of your notebook. Add new terms to it as they come up in assignments and in class. Use this list as a study tool for test review.

Pay special attention to textbook illustrations or drawings on handout sheets. These may turn up unlabeled on a science test, and you will have to write in the labels.

Tactics, Tips, and Traps

- The majority of questions you will be asked on science exams are these:
    - What is the definition of a particular science term?
    - How does a certain structure work?
    - What is the structure part of?
    - Draw the structure or label a drawing of the structure.
- Try to relate scientific principles to something in your own experience. For example, if you are studying ecosystems in earth science, think about how animals, insects, and vegetation are related to one another right in your own backyard.

SOCIAL STUDIES TESTS

Preparation

Get an overview of the span of history you

are studying from the beginning of the year. Read your textbook's table of contents, headings, and subheadings periodically. Keep up a time line as you read along so that you get a sense of the chronology and causes and effects of the events you are studying.

Relate the facts and details you must learn to larger ideas, events, and themes. As you learn information, try to fit it into your time line or into some kind of chronological plan you have in your head. At review time, take special note of tables, charts, and maps that reinforce the larger framework of ideas.

Tactics, Tips, and Traps

- About a week before a social studies test, list, in a phrase, each of the main ideas you have studied. Then next to each item, jot down all the names, dates, places, and facts that tie in with the main idea. Use this list and your time line as your pre-test study aids. Have a friend or family member recite the main idea and see how many facts you can associate with it. (You can also do this on a tape recorder.)
- Think of various time periods as a story. Read novels that fictionalize events in the time period you are studying. Search for nuggets of information that show you how the "real" people lived during a particular historical time. This will make the period more memorable for you at review time.
- Read with a critical mind. The whys and wherefores of social studies are more sig-

nificant than the rote recitation of dates and names. Ask yourself what events caused others. What were the turning points?

- When you get your test in hand, write a mini-outline or chronological list of ideas and facts as a first step to answering a social studies essay question.
- When you answer essay questions, develop your ideas and supporting information in the same time sequence implied in the test question.

FOREIGN LANGUAGE TESTS

Preparation

When you first read passages in another language, skim the whole section to get a sense of what it is about. Don't get bogged down in the twists and turns of vocabulary and grammar; you'll get a better grasp of both if you read them within the context of a whole passage.

Search for words that look and mean the same in both English and the language you are studying. Do keep in mind, though, that some words look and sound alike in both languages but have entirely different meanings. "Bureau" in French means "desk" or "office" while in English it means "dresser" or "department."

Do your review work with a tape recorder. Always translate from English into the other language, not the other way around.

Read foreign editions of magazines, newspapers, and books. Go to foreign language films.

Many students who have trouble studying a foreign language spend too much time on single words and grammar rules, never getting the sense of the language as a larger, living entity. As in all courses, if you grasp the big picture first, you'll find it easier to fit in the smaller details when a test rolls around.

Tactics, Tips, and Traps

- Memorizing idioms is more productive than learning single words.
- You'll have trouble with the grammar of a foreign language if you haven't mastered the rules of English grammar first. Know the definitions and functions of basic grammatical terms: nouns, pronouns, verbs, articles, etc.
- On the translation portion of a foreign language test, teachers usually read the passage through once, then more slowly a second time. Be very alert to the first reading to get an overall sense of the passage. Then, on the second reading, you will have an easier time fitting in words, phrases, and sentences.

Chapter 6

HOW TO TAKE STANDARDIZED TESTS INCLUDING THE SAT

Standardized tests, including the SAT, measure something called *aptitude*, your innate ability to apply what you have learned to new problems. Such tests generally cover two areas: the verbal category, which tests your skill in reading and English; and the mathematical section, which tests your ability to deal with numbers. Reading comprehension, even in the mathematical portions of such tests, is a key factor in determining test scores.

In recent years, there has been a great deal of controversy about how effective coaching is in helping students score higher on the SAT. The conclusions, although still not resolved, seem to indicate that knowledge of test skills and practice in similar tests does raise the scores of test-takers by about ten points. While there is no substitute for the kind of steady learning that only years of study can provide, you can make the most of what you have learned by developing your skills in taking such tests.

Forget about cramming for standardized tests. The body of knowledge on which you will be tested can only be accumulated over years of schooling. Vocabulary and reading comprehension are heavily stressed on such tests, so do make sure that you keep up on your word lists and that you are a careful reader.

While there is some disagreement about the value of commercial SAT practice books that contain tests similar to those you will be taking, it does help you to see how directions are worded; how the test is organized; and how to use your time to advantage. Check your bookstore for workbooks that contain such test models, and, in the weeks before your scheduled SAT or standardized test, give yourself some practice in taking the tests.

Make sure you've eaten well and are well rested the day of the test. Bring at least four number two pencils with good erasers, your admission card, scratch paper, and a good wristwatch to the test. Arrive in plenty of time so that you don't feel rushed. Sit near the front of the room, if possible, so that you can hear the test announcements clearly. If there is anything you feel confused about, ask questions before the test begins, since you won't be allowed to do so once the test is underway. Find out whether there is a penalty for guessing and whether you can return to incomplete sections.

Decide beforehand that you will make a schedule and stick to it; that you will use all the time you have; and that you will proofread your paper at least once.

Tactics, Tips, and Traps:
Standardized Tests

- Make sure you read the directions at least twice, underlining such key words as *true/false*, *least/most*, *smallest/largest*, etc.
- Take a minute to scan the whole section you have to work on to get a sense of what it covers.
- Schedule your time by dividing the number of minutes you have by the number of questions you have to answer. Leave a couple minutes per section for proofreading.
- Work on the easiest examples first. Mark those you plan to return to.
- Read each question at least twice, underlining or circling key words as you do so. Know exactly what you are expected to do.
- Don't jump to conclusions. Standardized test questions are carefully constructed so that each word really counts.
- Work quickly but carefully, making sure you don't spend more than your allotted time on any one question.
- Tackle the hard questions once you have completed the easy ones. Make sure you erase any stray marks on your paper. These exams are scored by machines that are sensitive to any pencil marks.
- Reason through the hard questions by rephrasing in your own words, using context clues, eliminating obviously wrong choices, and taking logical, shrewd guesses if you won't be heavily penalized for doing so.

- From time to time, check your question sheet against your answer sheet to make sure that you have left blanks in the places where you skipped questions.
- Proofread each section as you finish it. Make sure you have answered every question you intended to answer, that you marked each answer clearly, that you left no stray marks on the paper.

Tactics, Tips, and Traps: Reading Comprehension Sections

- The passages you are asked to read are generally organized around one main idea or theme. Each supporting paragraph presents a secondary idea related to the main theme. To boil down the passage to its basics:

  1. Read the passage once to get a sense of the whole.
  2. Read it a second time, looking for the main idea. Underline or circle it. Underline or circle supporting ideas as well.
  3. On your scratch paper, write a word or phrase that sums up the main idea. Below that, write a word or phrase that supports it. While these steps sound complicated, they should only take about two or three minutes and will help you keep your focus on the passage so that you don't have to waste time rereading it a third time.
  4. Answer the question. Read each of the choices carefully by underlining the

key words. Eliminate choices if they don't apply to the main idea of the selection, if they offer misinformation, or if they seem different in tone from the feeling of the passage.

- There are three main types of reading comprehension questions:
  1. Questions that really ask about the main idea. For example: "What title best expresses the theme of this selection?"; "This story may be described as . . ."; "This passage illustrates . . ."; "The writer's main theme is . . ."
  2. Questions that ask you about details. If you are expected to answer about facts from the passage, go back and circle important details before you write your answer.
  3. Questions that ask you to infer certain conclusions about the passage. Key words in inference questions are: *infers, suggests, indicates, apparently, seems to, probably, might, most likely,* and *because.* In these kinds of questions about a passage, the reason or meaning is not found directly in the selection itself, and you have to figure it out from the given information.
  4. Questions that ask you about the tone and style of the passage. This is a kind of inference question, since you have to determine what mood you think the author intended. The clues are the author's descriptive words and narrative comments.

Tactics, Tips, and Traps: Verbal Aptitude Sections

- You will find that most questions on the verbal aptitude or vocabulary section of a standardized test asks you to find one of the following:
    1. words that are the same in meaning (synonyms)
    2. words that are opposite in meaning (antonyms)
    3. the missing word that logically completes a statement
    4. words that are analogous (have the same relationship)
- Read the instructions carefully to determine just what you are supposed to be looking for.
- Be alert to choices that sound like the word in the question, e.g., *fulminate* means nearly the same as (a) *fumigate,* (b) *explode,* (c) *full-bodied,* (d) *betray.* The answer is *explode,* but *fumigate* and *full-bodied* are included among the choices as distractors. Be alert to this trap.
- If you can't find the choice that fits the word in the question, even when you know the meaning of the word, try to remember if the word has another meaning. The word *crest,* for example, can mean: *comb or tuft; top of a helmet; top of a hill; top of a wave; symbol of a family or institutional name.* Use the context (surrounding) words in the question or answer choices to determine what use is intended.

- Word analogies ask you to analyze parallel relationships between two pairs of words. These questions test your reasoning ability and word knowledge. Examples: *train:track* as *bus:road*. The connection here shows a vehicle in relation to its traveling surface. To complete analogies, figure out the relationship in the first pair. Here are some relationship types that frequently pop up on standardized tests:

word:synonym	(heartache:sorrow)
word:antonym	(happiness:sadness)
whole:to its part	(body:hand)
cause:effect	(fire:burn)
object:purpose	(mitt:catch)
raw material:product	(wood:table)
individual:group	(poodle:dog)
male:female	(rooster:hen)
noun:adjective	(country:countrified)
singular:plural	(goose:geese)

  Look for grammatical and logical clues in figuring out analogies.

Tactics, Tips, and Traps: Mathematical Standardized Tests

- Again, as in verbal sections of standardized tests, each and every word in the directions and questions counts. Read each question twice, underlining key words and phrases as you go along.
- In the problem-solving section, follow these steps:
  1. Quickly read the question to determine the subject and purpose of the problem.

2. Reread the question to find key word and to determine the extent and limits of the problem.
3. Cross out distractors (obviously wrong choices).
4. Rephrase the problem in your own words.
5. Decide how to solve the problem and what rules, formulas, or principles will help you to do so.
6. Apply the rules, formulas, and related principles as you work out the problem.
7. Review and recheck each step you used to solve the problem.

Appendix 1

TEST PREPARATION CHECKLIST

☐ Ask your teacher what will be covered on the test.

☐ Find out what kind of test will be given: objective (true-false, multiple-choice, matching, fill-in); or essay (long or short).

☐ Listen for clues from your teacher during the days or weeks before the test.

☐ Set up a study schedule to prepare for any big test:

    ☐ First, catch up on missing assignments; clear up.

    ☐ Get your notes in order.

    ☐ Look over old tests or talk to people who have taken tests in your course before.

    ☐ Make up study aids (lists of main ideas, definition sheets, outlines, summaries, time lines, etc.).

- [ ] Two nights before the test reread or memorize important material; review all your class notes and study aids; do memory work of facts, dates, rules, etc.
- [ ] Get all the materials you'll need for the test — pens, pencils, erasers, scratch paper, a wristwatch; anything else your teacher said to bring in. . . .

Get a good night's sleep.

Appendix 2

TEST STUDY SCHEDULE

Use this plan as a model for scheduling your study time before a big test.

Three weeks before the test:

Sunday	Monday	Tuesday	Wednesday

Thursday	Friday	Saturday

Two weeks before the test:

Sunday	Monday	Tuesday	Wednesday

Thursday	Friday	Saturday

One week before the test:

Sunday	Monday	Tuesday	Wednesday

Thursday	Friday	Saturday

TEST-TAKING CHECKLIST

☐ Be on time and well equipped for the test.
☐ Listen carefully to your teacher's comments. Find out if you will be penalized for wrong answers.
☐ Skim the test once to get a sense of what it covers.
☐ Read the directions twice, underlining key words on your second reading. Determine:
- the amount of time you have for the entire test and each of its sections.
- the point value of the questions.
- the number of compulsory questions.
- the style in which you are to answer the questions.

- ☐ Quickly figure out a schedule for the test and write it down on your scratch paper or somewhere on the test sheet. Divide the number of minutes you have for the test by the number of questions on the test, leaving five minutes for proofreading.
- ☐ Read each question twice, underlining key words as you do so.
- ☐ Do the easiest, most valuable questions first. Put a check mark next to those you plan to return to later on.
- ☐ Guess answers if only right answers are counted.
- ☐ Proofread your test to make sure you have completed all the examples. Reread the directions to determine if you have fulfilled all the requirements. Make sure matters of grammar, punctuation, and spelling are in order.
- ☐ Save your corrected test when you get it back and use it as a study aid for the next test.

Appendix 4

OUTLINE FORM

TOPIC: _____

I. _____
    A. _____
        1. _____
        2. _____
    B. _____
        1. _____
        2. _____

II. _____
    A. _____
        1. _____
        2. _____
    B. _____
        1. _____
        2. _____

III. _____
    A. _____
        1. _____
        2. _____
    B. _____
        1. _____
        2. _____

I. _____
    A. _____
        1. _____
        2. _____
    B. _____
        1. _____
        2. _____

II. _____
    A. _____
        1. _____
        2. _____
    B. _____
        1. _____
        2. _____

III. _____
    A. _____
        1. _____
        2. _____
    B. _____
        1. _____
        2. _____

Appendix 5

TEST RECORD SHEET

Course	Type of Test	Date

Grade	Strong and Weak Points

Course	Type of Test	Date

Grade	Strong and Weak Points

INDEX